TO HELL AND BACK

The life account of Jason Murra

By: Jason Murra

iUniverse, Inc.
New York   Bloomington

iUniverse books may be ordered through booksellers or by contacting:

iUniverse
1663 Liberty Drive
Bloomington, IN 47403
www.iuniverse.com
1-800-Authors (1-800-288-4677)

Because of the dynamic nature of the Internet, any Web addresses or
links contained in this book may have changed since publication and
may no longer be valid. The views expressed in this work are solely those
of the author and do not necessarily reflect the views of the publisher,
and the publisher hereby disclaims any responsibility for them.

ISBN: 978-1-4401-5981-7 (sc)
ISBN: 978-1-4401-5982-4 (ebook)

Printed in the United States of America

iUniverse rev. date: 10/26/2009

I would like to thanks my kids. Thank you, for without you, I would never have made it. We have been through a lot. I love you. Dad

I would also like to thank Dave Warmuth for taking the pictures that are on my book.

I would also like to thank the rock group KISS for I inspiring me to believe in myself, and dreams really do come true. ACE, GENE, PETER, and PAUL, thank you so much.

.

I sit the night and stare. The mirror tells me lies. It makes me be things I don't want. It lives inside my mind. Will this thing crush my soul, or let me live in peace? Is it trying to get out? Or burrowing inside of me?
Jason Murra 1985

The hatred it burn inside my eyes. The fear it lives inside my head. I heave a high depressive sigh and hope that I would die. I wish my fears would come to pass and not fade like all of my dreams.

Jason Murra 1987

Table of Contents

Chapter one:
Earliest Memories.

It was a cold dark snowing night in Iron Mountain in 1968, to the family of William Murra was born a son Jason Paul Murra. At first my name was to be Christopher Noel Murra, but my parents later decided to call me Jason Paul. I was the last of five children, otherwise known as the baby of the family. I don't remember too much until around the age of three is where my earliest memories are. I can remember sliding down the stairs with my niece Deanna and also playing wit h a toy airplane outside. I remember my first spring, making mud pies from all the melting snow. Life was fun at that age, but then who can argue since as a child you don't know any better. I can some what remember playing with my brothers. We would run around out house playing with our toys. I had two brothers and two sisters. I don't remember my sisters living at home only my two brothers. My mom had me at an older age 38 years old. It was a long time after I was born, that I found out my mom really didn't want me.

My parents grew up in Iron Wood, Michigan; at that time my dad had been working for OK Auto Supply. That is where he sold automobile parts, and he worked there until his retirement in 1990. M mother worked for J. C. Penney's selling clothing. They both went to Catholic School, where they met, and got married. We just celebrated their 50th Wedding Anniversary two years ago, and all of the wedding party came. I know my dad was in WWII on the ship called the Indianapolis. For a short time he was away.

In 1950 my parents moved to Iron Mountain because my dad got transferred from his job in Iron Wood to Iron Mountain. My father was an auto parts man for 48 years of his life. It is now 2007, a far time from when I started this chapter. Since then I have been able to unlock certain memories that have been repressed for many years. I think you will find them disturbing, humorous, and serious as well. It is true that I don't have a lot of memories from this house, but I certainly can share a few. I remember the time when my older brother had a tree house in the front yard. He had fallen out of it, and he broke his collar bone. The ambulance had to come and get him, and I was very scared. I remember crying and my oldest sister had taken me and lay with me on the couch and I fell asleep. I remember one time my mom had bought each of the boys a numbered shirt. I was so proud of that shirt; I kept looking at the big number on it. Another time I remember was my oldest brother had a dirt bike. This neighbor kid was trying to ride it and couldn't work the clutch. We had gone in, and I had gone back outside to play on it. He had come around the corner and I said "this is how you do it" and he punched me in the stomach. I remember walking around picking up piles of beer cans, and having large piles.

In 1972 I can remember when the City of iron Mountain had built the 25 Play Ground. There used to be a gang around our area called the 25 Gang. The play ground area consisted of a tennis court and a children's play ground. I remember my older brother and me hiding in the holes in the ground where the cement forms were to be poured. We would stick our heads up to see if anyone was peeking first. I remember the downstairs had a bar and a shower, and up stairs had a cubby room. I remember there was an old man who lived behind us. He had lost his leg I believe because of WWI. He was nice to me and would give me candy bars. I do remember one time when my parents bought me a Tonka truck, which was a grader. This is where I can remember my earliest bout with depression.

Chapter two:
Living with the life I have

In the summer of 1973, my father wanted to move out in the country, I was told the reason why we moved was to go snowmobiling, but in true fact it was because my mom was fighting and driving the neighbors crazy. He bought a house not too far from town, but yet it was in a country like setting. I never knew that when I moved, I would not see the friends that I have made living in town. It was a totally new experience for me. I had to adjust to not having friends around like I used to. A lot of fun I made was with me. It was around this time when I started to become depressed, (even to say the earliest memories) I think a lot of it had to do with being isolated. I know my mother surely was depressed, she would cry and cry from being lonely. I remember many times she would throw stuff at my dad asking "why did we move here"?

Going to school was ok, I remember my first day for some reason I missed the bus that was to take me to school, so the custodian had to bring me there. That is where I met Charlie, the bus driver. He became my somewhat type of friend that I could talk to. He always seemed to be crabby to the other kids on the bus, but not to me.

Life for me was hard, especially to breathe. I never knew what was wrong, my parents would bring me to the allergist in Green Bay, but he was more worried about my skin rashes than my breathing. Every week I would get allergy shots. Then one day in 1974, I had seen a commercial for Primatene Mist. I told my mom to buy it for me, it really helped me to breathe, and it was later that I found out that I have asthma. Even to this day if my mom hadn't bought me that medicine, I don't think I would be around to tell every one about my story. During my younger years, I was closer to my mom than to my dad. It was only recently 1991, that I started to have a relationship with him. I believe it has to do with me having kids, and it actually wasn't mine; it was my ex – wife's kids. When we would come over to his house for whatever reason, he would love up those kids so much; that's what brought us together.

Growing up with my siblings was ok. I don't remember too much of my sisters being around, since they were much older than I, but I do remember growing up with my two brothers. When I was younger, my oldest brother would take me fishing a lot and we would go for rides on his motor bike. It was always a great treat when school got out, he would take me to the local restaurant to a farmer's omelet. He would always look over my report card and decide if I was worth taking to the restaurant. The middle brother, (he is the tyrant of the family) we never got along when we were younger, he would always beat me up, I think that he was jealous that I was the youngest of than the family and not him. My oldest sister I always had a very good time with, there been many numerous times I would be with her, even though I was scared to stay at her house. This did get better with time and I always wanted to live with her. I guess that I thought of her more as my mom than as my sister. She would take me over to her friend's house. She would always around Christmas time go to the parade and meet Santa. I guess she was my escape from the bad times I had at home. If it wouldn't have been for her giving me all those experiences, I would have never known what I would have missed. My parents never gave me those experiences as a normal child would have. My sister Tiny I have never had a relationship and we barely even talk. I used to live next to her and in the four years that we lived by each other, she only came by once. I can't say all bad things about her; at least she was nice to my kids. And it wasn't until just recently; I have been seeing her more than any of my other siblings. We have some personal things in common, which has rekindled our friendship. After going to college I really must say that I came from quite a dysfunctional and separated family. Like I said I noticed that I suffered from depression, I guess that's why I tried to kill myself in the third grade. Nobody done nothing about it, even my brother just made fun of me. From that day fourth I have lived a life of having a loaded gun at my head. Always thinking suicidal, I often wonder if it had to do with the abuse from my mother. I remember watching my dad walking back to work and I had my hands on the window saying "Daddy don't go" and she grabbed me saying "come here you son of a bitch". I know that there is more abuse, I have just suppressed it. Growing up I was always scared of things. I remember when I was sent to West Wood School I has paranoid feelings about being there, smells of the school made me scared. I was scared of being beaten up by other kids. I remember my parents driving by it and I started to panic and cry. In the third grade, I missed 68 days of school, mostly due to being scared. It wasn't all bad though, it was 1976 and hey KISS was the band. A really cool kid; Bob was into KISS too and we would go to the West Wood market every day to read the 16 magazine , Cream, Star, Teen, and all the other magazines that had KISS in them, oh and we bought quite a few too and we would exchange pics and posters. There was a teacher there named Mr. Bauer, I really liked him, he actually knew of my asthma problems, and I can't remember if he had actually bought me an asthma inhaler or not, but when I needed to use it. He would keep it in his desk. I did. Bless his soul. Growing up trying to do any kind of sports was not even capable due to my condition. I did try basket ball in the seventh grade. I did one game and I had to quit. My older brother was an ass hole to me about playing sports. He would make fun of my asthma making wheezing noises and talking like my mom saying" oh he has asthma". There will be more on him don't worry. As I said I was really scared about that school. I just was paranoid of the looks of it, the smells of it, even the teachers, I remember this one teacher Mrs. Demerse wow was she a jerk. I don't know for sure but the story goes that one day I went to school with dirty arms and she called social services on my parents. My mom was mad and had me yanked out of west wood and put me into Catholic School. But before we go there, have something to say. My parents are devout Catholics and of course I had to go to CCD. I hated it I had no respect, and I was kicked out on numerous occasions, I think that's why I was put in to Catholic School. I still don't know how I went from the third grade after missing 68 days to the fourth grade. Catholic School was Hell in its own. I didn't get along with too many kids there they hated me. Only the outcasts were the ones that I got along with. I was there for fourth grade, fifth, and part of sixth grade when I was kicked out. I hated this school so bad I couldn't stand it. Can you believe that in the fourth grade, when the bus would drop me off at school I would just turn around and walk home. Yea that's right I would skip school, many times a week. I was sometimes driven back, but I would just leave again. There is this one teacher Mary Brien. I can't wait till the day she dies. I want to go to her funeral and

P.P. and spit on her corpse. This jerk had me scoped out in front of the other kids. She tortured me, ridiculed me, belittled me, made me look stupid, and made me look filthy. Every day she would make me get up in front of the class and go to the bathroom and wash my hands. It was hard for me to do any work, and whenever I made a mistake, she was sure let the class know of how stupid I was. I had many times of wanting to go to school with a special gun we had that held a 25 round clip and just going to town on her and some kids. Looking back at this, and knowing what I know now. I understand what a kid must be going through to commit a school shooting. I also hated most of the kids there, being picked on among other things made me not to want to go. I had a really fun time with this kid named Tom. We had fun I remember one time we were given and assignment in English Class to do a commercial. During this time we were listening to an album called Cheech & Chongs Los Togino we did a commercial for gonorrhea we didn't know what in the hell it meant and it sounded funny to us. When we did it, we got ourselves sent to the office. Of course I've been sent to the office many times. A lot of times were to "take my pill" (Ritalin). I would never take, I would just go from the first floor to the second and throw it on the ground and I would crush it. It was really funny they had to check my mouth to see if I swallowed it. I also spent many days after school because of the trouble I would get in. I remember one time a friend of mine and I decided to break into the school. We picked the door and it opened. Once inside we had a feast of destruction. It was a fifth grade teacher's room, he loved the Detroit Lions, we just smashed and busted up everything he had. That was pretty much what we did to most of the rooms. One thing I thought was cool was music class. This teacher was nice to me. She actually let me bring in records to play for music. Records like: KISS, AC DC, and Queen just to name a few. I have to say that I can remember skipping school and walking home to see my mom sitting the kitchen table drinking beer. It was my mother who had given me my first beer. One day when I came home, she took me down town to buy me a pipe and some pipe tobacco. Being able to drink at home was morally accepted, and smoking too. My parents bought me numerous cans of chew to say the least. One of my first cans was the happy days mint chew. I don't think they make that brand anymore. I remember one day in 1980, I decided to stay home from school I wanted to go ice fishing. I grabbed a six pack of Old Milwaukee and headed out. I was introduced to alcohol at a young age. I also can remember in Catholic School, my oldest sister had used to take me to Green Bay for allergies and asthma maintenance. I have said it once and I will say it again, I have always thought of her as my mom rather than my sister. I really hated being at home, especially when my parents would fight and argue. Well one last thing on Catholic School. One day this one kid was picking on me to the point that I grabbed him by the throat. I must have held on long enough that the teacher stepped in when I lost my grip he went to the floor choking and coughing. I was kicked out of school, never to return.

When I started 7th grade, I didn't quite know what to expect. I felt scared, but I knew the first two weeks of school were kind of lax. It didn't take too long for me to find myself hanging out with the "burn outs" as they were called. A burn out was mostly a person who smoked cigarettes, and drank alcohol and would normally skip school. There were quite a few burn outs in the 7th grade. I did feel a little bit better than being at Catholic school. I wasn't really picked on or at least that I can remember. Being at home scared me, I remember one day when I came home with my report card, and my mom was on the front porch telling me to run away your older is going beat you up for having bad grades. I remember running towards the train tracks behind my house and I hid. I can't quite remember for how long, but I remember being scared as shit of him. And being scared of him was an every day event. I have always had to worry about my brother hurting me and my mom. One time he lost some concert tickets and wanted my mom to pay for some new ones. The whole day was hell, I think I'd of been better off going to school. He came after us and I took the key to the bathroom, which I locked. He tried to come in by kicking the door. I've had many times to worry about what he was going do to me. All too often it was an every day event. Now I know I told you that I had asthma, but I know that you never knew I had eczema, which is a bad skin rash. I mostly wore long sleeved shirts because the rash was on the inside bends of my arms, on the back side of my knees, and on my feet. I really hated gym class, not only because it was hard for me to participate because of the asthma, but because of the embarrassment of the skin rash. Luckily it went away at the end of the 7th grade. My dad always said it would go away and it did. My dad wasn't always the best with me either, he would call me stupid, dumb. One time a friend Kurt and I had an ice shack on Lake Antoine, we had left all of our fishing stuff in it from the previous night. The next day, when he dropped us off he was going to pick us up during his lunch hour. We shortly found out, we had our shack broken into. We took it apart and when he got back to get us. We asked him to wait; he said "no I have to go to work" and left us there. It was very cold, below zero weather. We started to walk back, after a while an older man that we knew Mr. Wilson had stopped and offered us a lift to my house. When ever Kurt and I went fishing, we had beer. One time in 7th grade we fished Bass Lake we had about eight bottles of Buck Horn Beer in one of those old types of beer cases. We caught a ton of perch and we just stuck them into the case along with the empties. We must have had 50 fish. Kurt was about the only friend I had that understood what it was like to grow up in a fucked up house. Whenever he would stay over, my mom would have got us beer to drink. One time she even bought us a bottle of Schnapps. I can remember even in grade school around 4th grade I can remember Kurt and me taking our bikes and just roaming Iron Mountain. The Camelot Video Arcade was a real cool place to hang out. I especially liked to see the KISS Pinball Machine.

There were never any kids there our age at the time we went there. We would go all around the town. One time I was in 5th grade and I had left to go to Mr. Doughnuts around 11:00 a wind storm had came over the area, and when I went to ride my bike home, my dad had came to get me. I would have to say 7th grade was a little bit better. I remember for my birthday my mom bought me a 12 pack of Old Style. For that weekend, I pretty much stayed in my room.

My parents are lifetime members of The United Sportsmen's Club. They started to go there in 1974, and that is where I met a kid named Jim. We were somewhat friends. I remember my parents going up there on their snowmobiles. I always loved my mom's snowmobile, a 1972 Arctic Cat panther 303 Wankel. Man that was the coolest thing. They did a lot of snowmobiling when they were younger, but of course as they got older, time has a way of slowing you down. We always went to the club and always on the weekend. My parents would put on the motorcross races. That was always fun. Seeing all of the bikes was cool. I remember one time when I was a kid, I was down stairs and for no apparent reason, and this kid pulled a gun and put it to my head. He kept saying he was gonna kill me. It seemed like an eternity, but I guess it was no more that 10 minutes. I don't know what happened, but I knew that I was running upstairs to get my dad. My dad and a guy named Jim went down stairs and ripped this guy a new one. I also remember them putting on snowmobile races too. That was only a couple of them. It was fun going to weddings and dancing and not to mention the alcohol I could drink. At this time it was 1981, I had got my first job working for the Sportsmen's Club in the trap and skeet area. I was a trap boy and would load the skeet machine that throws out skeet to be shot at. This was also a dark time for me around 1980. I was in the chicken coop (my dad raised chickens) my oldest brother had made me pull down my pants. I remember him playing with my gentiles and then he done oral sex on me. I think it was done at least three times that I can remember. During my 8th grade year I remember him molesting me in a way he wanted me to perform oral sex on him, otherwise he wouldn't take me for a ride. This was also done a lot of times in his bed room. Then I remember him masturbating in front of me. He wanted me to see it and when he was done, he said "that's what makes the baby". NOBODY KNOWS OF THIS, NOT EVEN MY MOM AND DAD. I WANTED TO WAIT UNTIL IT WAS RIGHT TO COME OUT WITH THIS. One of the reasons why I wrote this book was to get this off of my chest and I think it's time my family members knew about it. Being in 8th grade was ok too. I caused some problems and got kicked out. I used to get sick a lot and I hated to call my mom to come home because I knew my brother was there home doing nothing. He had quit school and even though I was sick, he made me clean the house. That was one thing about living with an alcoholic; you always have to do the house work. I cleaned everything and did the laundry too. It really sucked. Not only was it hard to have some one come over for fear of my parents start bitching, but a dirty house as well. It really pissed me off to see her just sitting there drinking beer, reading a bible, and listening to music. Oh and nothing was more degrading as when you had some one over and you were walking to the kitchen and she says "stop, stop!" That meant she was taking a piss in a pail in the kitchen. Then when she's done, she takes it out the back door and dumps it off the side of the porch. Then around noon or one O'clock she goes to bed until 4:00 to start supper. Then my dad comes home and they start fighting all night. It really tore me to hell when she would call my dad a dumb pecker, or "why did you have to make the last kid?" I was the last kid. She even said "you had to use your tool hey dumb pecker"? I guess that is why I tried to commit suicide in the 3rd grade. Everything that I have just told you had happened every night, it never failed. My oldest brother always used to tell me that "mom and dad are going to leave one day and never come back". I learned that from being told this when I was young; this is why I fear that people want to leave me. My eldest brother also used to pull my hair a lot when he got mad too. I'm not sure why he was mad at me. It really sucked not having a birthday with kids. I'm 38 years old and this is why I am writing this book. I hope it is to let you know what I went through, and it is a source of healing for me, and I hope it is a source of healing for you too. In 8th grade I did have a friend. I slept over his house. We did drink. His name was Devin. Even though alcohol was involved I didn't care it was too late in my life to think it was wrong. After all I only started to smoke pot in the 5th grade. Devin was like a big brother to me. The only irony about our friendship is he was 8 years older than me. We would always go out cruising and boozing. He taught me the ways of the land, to hunt and fish, and to have an appreciation for the out doors. Maybe that is why I have started a duck club. There will be more on this in another chapter. 8th grade was pretty much like the 7th grade. One time I had a beer party at my house. There was about six of us kids drinking and smoking. We had the stereo cranked just having a good time. Around 1:00 after everyone had left, Kurt and I decided to take my snowmobile for a ride. We were just plowed going as fast as the machine would go. As we went down the road, I lost control of the sled. We went side ways and we hit an electric pole. When we got up I had smashed off the skis, and we started to laugh about it. Holy fuck man did you see that? I asked him. We drove the machine back to my house as Kurt held on to the skis. We went to bed. When we woke, we went out side to check out the sled. Not only was the skis gone, but I busted a motor mount. That following week at school, there was a lot of talk about the party, and I remember talking to Kurt about smashing the snowmobile. The principal heard what I had said he said" I am going to call your parents and tell them all that happened". I said go ahead. I don't know if he did, but I never heard of it. Little did I know it, but my alcoholism was escalating. On May 31, 1983 was one of the worst days of my life. One of my best friends had committed suicide. That sunk me into a deep depression. I will tell you more about this later.

Wow! Well here I am in 9th grade and hot to trot. At this time my dad had bought me a new Suzuki 4 wheeler. I think it was more like a baby sitter than a toy. Being a freshman wasn't scary for me. At least I don't remember. I remember getting ready for my first hour class. It was art and as I walked to the room, there was a kid holding some KISS pictures. I asked him if I could take a look at them. He didn't mind. I gave them back and then he was in the same class as I was in. his name was Don. He was a really great kid. We had a super relationship. We had our fill of good beer and laughing. I remember we always made fun of people in the school. Another guy Stan was a cool kid too. We would go out at lunch time and smoke pot in the parking lot. I don't know if it's the pot or what, but I can't remember too much about the 9th grade; maybe it was due to the fact I had a concussion. One day I had got really intoxicated. I went to class, it was math I my memory serves me right, well I sat in the back row, which those were regular seats. I remember sitting back or leaning as you call, I had passed out and then all the sudden, wham! I fell completely back hitting my head. I remember the class laughing, but when I got up I stumbled and hit the floor unconscious. That's all I remember. I guess the ambulance had got me and took me to the hospital. I was in there for three days. I had bruised my brain. Ever since, I always seem to loose my balance and I get light headed. I am sure this is something I will live with for the rest of my life. Now back to my art projects and my friends. I do know that every art project I made had to do with KISS. Dave did the same. In 1984, we all went to see Kiss play in Marquette. That was a fun concert to go on. Loud music, pot and beer made for a great combination. There was this one guy who was in a wheel chair. People actually picked him up and got him on stage next to Kiss. I bet that was a real rush for him. We had seen Kiss before in Milwaukee that was awesome too. You know the stuff we did as teens;

I couldn't imagine my kids doing. With the fines and things you have to do. I hope my kids don't read this book; I don't want them getting any ideas. They have no idea what kind of a person I was. It was always fun going to a concert because that meant usually skipping school. In 9th grade was fun for me. I got a job at the Big Boy Restaurant as a dish washer. I met a couple of kids there too. We would go up to my camp with a barrel and get totally drunk all weekend. I can't remember how this started, but I was able to buy beer in Wisconsin. Almost every weekend, we would get a barrel and strap it to my 4 wheeler and head to camp in Sagola. There would be around seven of us. We all had bikes which was cool. I am trying to keep names to a minimum. Like I said camp was fun as hell. This was also the time when we started to find other party places. Bad Waters was an awesome place to party. The cops never bothered us. As the year progressed, we started to get more people coming to the camp. It was getting to the point that older kids in cars were coming. There were many times that both sides of the road were filled with cars.

I do remember some fights, but that was taken out side. Boy, I'm having a hard time trying to remember certain events. I remember one time mark and I took our bikes and we stole a bunch of the blinking construction lights. We shut the lights off in the camp. We were all laughing man was that fun. I remember one time that Glen had a big red my dad bought me one too. It had to been around 2:00 AM and we needed some fire wood, so we decided to steal some. We drove the bikes into Sagola and at this gas station there was some wood. We filled up, but first we stopped at the Ace of Clubs Bar.

We had a drink and went on our way. It was two miles from the junction to the camp. Around one mile down the road, I noticed Glen was veering to the left. Now I was a little bit behind him, but soon he went left into the ditch flew in the air and landed into a swamp with cat tails. Glen fell asleep at the wheel on his ATV. We laughed about that for many years. All the bikes my dad bought me I had: 1984 Suzuki, 1985 Yamaha 225 DX, Kawasaki Tecate, and 1984 Honda Big Red. Every one of them bikes I have smashed. I remember one time I had my girlfriend Mary on the back of my bike. We were riding hard and fast hitting a lot of bumps. I feel so bad that I messed up her back. I have not seen her in a long time, I hope you are ok. Then there was this one time in 1984 during deer season. I know you who are reading this book remember Ray. He and I hung out a lot too. I even lived at his house. Well he was up at camp with me. On opening night I shot a spike. We got it back, and done all we needed to do. We drank straight and heavy. It was around 11:00 and we decided to take the bikes for a ride. Honestly we were six sheets to the wind it was snowing and I decided to do some fish tailing. Now don't ask me why but I decided to wear a helmet. As I was fish tailing going fast, my tire caught a hard dry piece of road. I flipped upside down still holding on to the handle bars. When all of the sudden the bike fell and dropped on top of me. I got up and checked to see if the bike was ok, Ray grabbed my helmet it was cracked at the back. Styrofoam was showing through. Can you imagine if I didn't wear a helmet that night? That was a fun deer season in 1984. Ray and I had planned it for weeks. I burrowed a trailer from Scott, so we could put our stuff in there. When we left, we went and got a twelve pack of beer for the ride. We left Tuesday night and didn't come back until Sunday after noon. My dad was there, my middle brother was there and acting like a dick head as usual swearing at me, and personally degrading me in front of my friend. When we would have parties at camp, if my brother would show up, my friends and I would leave. One thing that was odd was we never got corrected as kids, never a spanking, punishment, or grounding of any kind. I remember the first time I went to Don's house was cool. I was such a thrill to see all of the Kiss Posters he had collected. We also played guitar he was lead and I was bass. When his parents were gone, we would get some friends over and drink and play guitars. We had a three piece band at one time. Don on lead, Stan on drums, and me on bass, But we were the band that wasn't to be. I used to stay at his house a lot I remember I was just falling asleep when Don's mom and dad came home she said we both smell like a couple of pot factories. We just laughed the next day. Don had a really cool car a 1975 Mercury Monarch. He souped it up and it had a high rear end. Man that was a sweet car. We used to run the pavement until the tires would fall off.

Tenth grade was my worst year in school thus far. I was in a deep, deep depression that whole year. I was still working in the restaurant. I was always thinking of committing suicide, I had tried it many times. My home life wasn't very good. As a matter of fact, I had left home to go and live with Ray. At least there I knew I was safe. Ray had a really nice 3 wheeler; a 200X Honda. Ray and I would cruise the trails around our area. We used to buy a lot of pot and smoke it along the trails as well as drink. I had met this girl Rochelle, and after school I would go to her house, and pick her up and go to my parent's house to screw away. There was one time that Ray and I had gone to this chick's house over by Moon Lake. She was having a party and we had stopped at the liquor store to buy a case, and I bought a bottle of Jack Daniels. When we got to the party my friend Don and Stan were there too. I remember taking that bottle of Jack and just drinking it straight like kool aide. Don and I had to do a beer run, so we got on my Yamaha and headed for Wisconsin. I knew I was pretty fucked up and when I got in there I was yelling Happy New Year. I knew I was bad because Don wanted to drive and I let him. Ray stayed after I decided to leave. When I left sherry was out side. I was acting like a show off revving the bike, I popped the clutch and I flipped right upside down. Every thing was so dizzy. They helped me get my bike up right and off I went. I went to my house and when I got inside, I turned on the kitchen light, and I vomited up in the kitchen sink. My dad had gotten up. He looked at me, and then went back to bed. I went back into my bed and went asleep. When I woke up, I left for Ray's house. He told his mom that I wanted to go to my house for the night. His parents were so nice, they bought me new clothes, and they really took good care of me. I am so glad for them; I have a goal to search for them on the internet. If there was anybody who was a normal influence, it was them. I remember one time, we went to play racquet ball. I played, but remember I have asthma, and boy did I pay for it. I was so happy to get to their house, so I could use my inhaler.

School wasn't fun for me either; this was my worst year of all time. I really thought about quitting school, but for some reason I never did that. I was suspended a couple of times, One time I had put a teacher in the head lock, and I brought him to the ground. A teacher from the next room heard the commotion, and he kicked me. I did let go, but I was suspended. Another time, with the same teacher, I chased him down to the principal's office. I wanted to hurt him so bad. Then one time, this one kid had wanted me to move to another seat. I said no. he pushed and then I got up and grabbed him by the throat, and I punched him right in the face. One teacher told me that "I was going to have a rough life because of my attitude". Do you know that statement has still stuck to me this very day? One day I had a very bad day at school, I was really depressed, and I wanted to go home. I went into Mr. Mariaunna's office and I said I wanted to go home. He asked "what's the matter you are sick"? No I replied. "Then what is it"? I said I wanted to go home and kill myself. He was really scared, he phoned my parents and shortly before you know it, I was at the counseling center. This was my first time talking to some one about my problems. I started going there once a week. I don't remember the guy's name, but he was really cool. We started to build a friendship, we would exchange cassette tapes. That was fun. I really liked going there; he was like my special friend. It all shattered one day when my brother sat down at the supper table and started yelling at me saying, "I don't want to hear about guns, do I have to take them away? You know Devin killed himself. He is in Hell. That's what happens if you kill yourself". My brother always had a good way of degrading me in front of people at any given moment. He thinks he is helping me, but all what he was really doing was making me hurt even more. Some of the worst things were when he was hitting my mom, and I was so scared, I would run to my room and hide. The violence continued pretty much on a daily basis. He kept hitting her until 1992, which wasn't that long ago. The last thing I heard is he had kicked her in her fake hip. By that time, I had moved out of the house. This was the first year that I got kicked out of school for putting a teacher in the head lock. I chased a teacher down the hall.

As I have said this year was my worst. I am sure that I must have had a nervous break down, I just didn't know it. People just never liked me for who I was, I think some of it had to do with my brother blasphemy of me to other kids at school. On the last day of school, I had bought a new record at the store and I wanted to take it home to play. That made me feel good, when I got home my brother yelled at me and told me that life isn't about music.

The11 grade:

This year for some reason was a good year for me. It actually started with my friend Don picking up my report card from school and bringing it to where we worked. He said that Mr. Mariuanna had said that if I don't shape up I might as well not go to school. I made a goal for me to do better in school. And that is exactly what I did. I made the honor rolls for the first ½ of the year. It seems that I finally had what I wanted in life. Peace. For once in my life I felt a sense of respect. Even by the teachers. I had a lot of girls like me and ask me out in this year. You know I still drank and smoked pot. I remember one time, I was at this kid's house and his step dad was a Doctor. I told the kid I wanted to get some pot and he told me look into the freezer. It was like no way! Holy wow! I helped myself to a full large sized bag of pot with red hairs in it. I got it for free that was the best part. I will never reveal the name of the Doctor, so don't even bother asking. In this year, I had bought a hunting knife from a teacher. I still have it, but try to do that today. I even met a nice girl Sheba. She is in another chapter. I did well even though I did drugs. At lunch hour was the time to get high. We were in the chick's car, and we smoked a lot of joints, and when the door was opened, it just bellowed smoke. How funny. Now remember I said this was a good year. In the beginning it sort of wasn't let me back up. During around the first week of school, I was put at the Voc Center. They had put me into auto mechanics. I hated it. I was taking welding and I loved that, but I didn't like mechanics. I wanted to take machine tool. They told me there was no room. So I decided to quit school. I remember standing by the electronics room, and Mr. Justus was walking by and he asked me "what is the matter?" I told him I was quitting school. He said no you're not. He got me into machine tool and then like I said I had a great year. And one of the reasons why it was so great was because of Bob Justus. You see I loved welding; it was like my diamond in the rough. It made me feel important and needed. I was a really good welder. I have a lot of respect for Bob. He is gone now. But I can always remember chewing snuff in his class. I made a lot of projects, a lot of wood stoves stoves. I was even the teacher's assistant for the night school class. That was fun imagining me teaching people. I got a nice certificate for that. Even though I was drinking and doing drugs, I was Flying High Again.

12 Th grade:

This year was an up and down year for me. I felt really awesome because I was with this girl. I loved welding. And we had lots of good parties. I remember when Shelia took me clothes shopping, we had fun the first thing I bought was the new OZZY album. I had to get that before picking out clothes. For those of you who remember me, I had lots of albums at least 200. Well, they're all gone. I started selling them in 2004 thanks to EBAY. I only have a select few that I am still going to sell. I hope to get the negatives from a friend who took pictures of my room. Those that remember my room was immersed in KISS posters and you name it. I still have all of that stuff, although it is preserved in my basement. During this year, I had a strong desire to go into the service. I wanted to follow into my dad's footsteps, so I joined the Navy. This was like the pinnacle of my life. I had a girl, something I loved to do, and I was in the Navy. When my recruiter told me all of the things you can do in the service, I was pumped up. I had a girl, something I loved to do, and I was in the Navy. What could go wrong? Well reality set in. even though I signed up, when I went for my physical I was let go due to asthma problems. I guess good thing don't last forever. It finally dawned on me I couldn't be with Sheba any more either. You see not only couldn't I be in the service, but in reality welding; and breathing in all that smoke was not good for me either, besides the fact when I'd use my inhaler, I would shake like crazy and that does not make for a good welder. I know Sheba wanted to get married and have kids. I knew that I couldn't give her a life like she wanted. In time I started to detach myself from her. I started to party even more and with out her. I started to cheat on her. I remember one time my friend Glen and I were ice fishing. Sheba and a friend of hers came by to visit. We talked and she wanted to know if another person was going to come by. (I am trying to keep people innocent), I said maybe. I know it was sometime around or shortly after Christmas break that we broke up. That is when my life fell to the bottom. For the rest of the school year I was literally doing and drinking anything imaginable. I must say that I did have fun with her when we went to see Ted Nugent in Marquette that was a blast. And if any of my fellow class mates remember the famous "NUGENT KICKS ASS" shirt that I wore to school. That's where it came from. I will always remember Mr. Mack made me turn around every day in class, to make sure I wasn't wearing anything inappropriate. Now back to Sheba for one minute. I always loved her parents, we would go to their camp and her dad and I would get totally wasted. One time I was so drunk, I passed out at the table and her mom dragged me into bed. It was always fun going to Sheba's house because we got to go to bed together, her parents didn't mind. I remember her dad and I would go to Putzer's pot belly bar. He always got me drinks, and we would just love to fucking kill people at smear. We won lots of drinks that way. There were many nights we passed out together. I am forever grateful for her parents indeed.

One thing that I would really like to get off my chest one day in Art class, there was this one kid who was a smart ass. He wouldn't stop trying to tease me. Well on this day we had to leave the Art room to go to study hall. While we were walking down there, I had grabbed him by the throat and I literally lifted him off the floor. I just remember squeezing his throat hard. He started to tremble and his eyes rolled back, I then let him go. He was unconscious for about 30 seconds. I was really scared; I thought I had killed him. He lay motionless. As the kids gathered around, I remembered the study hall teacher saying "you are in a hell of a lot of trouble you know that"? I was freaking out. I killed someone, I pleaded with the Lord saying I won't do that ever again. Then all of the sudden he started to cough and he came back to. To this day I have never got into a fight with any one. And I hold my promise.

On the very last night of my senior year, Glen and my girlfriend I went out. We had bought a case of old style and a bottle of amaretto. We went on a long cruise, and that is just what we did. It must have been around 11:30, we were both drunk. And right by the City Park. I was driving and I wanted to make the balls big, so we went in the city park the wrong way. Well the cops were there. Glen was getting huffy with the cops; I don't quite understand the situation. I know I was drunk, but they never gave me a ticket. I know at the cop shop I took a breathalyzer, and I was like double drunk. The reason they let us go is because my girlfriend wasn't drunk. They took out beer. When we got out, we went and picked up a 12 pack. At this time my mom was mad when I got home, yelling. I just turned around with barb, and we spent the night at Glen's house. I remember when I went back to school for my last day, this counselor told me that I shouldn't hang out with Glen and Barb was bad news. I said "yea and like try to correct my life on the last day of school fucking ass hole". I went through school and made the most of my last day. I was happy because school was all over with. My friend Ken had spent the weekend at my house. We got totally wasted. We cruised and cruised in my car just having fun. On Sunday was graduation, I couldn't believe it, for I was finishing school. I just barely made it to graduate, but I did it. Kurt and I started drinking around 9: AM. We pulled my stereo speakers out my bedroom window and cranked up the jams. Man I felt like a million bucks, I was getting all this attention. All these relatives had come over, who some I'd not ever seen were wishing me a happy graduation and good luck. All I knew on that day is it was my day just for me. There was lots of people, and food, and beer. My dad had bought three kegs, and had two on reserve. All of the people who I hung out with were there before, and after the graduation. Graduation was exciting, but I'd never realize how much I miss my class mates later on in years to come. I friend of mine Krissie I always told her that when I graduated, I was going to hang my gown in the trees at school, and burn my gown. She always laughed about it. Well I never did it. My gown is still in my closet in my bed room at my parent's house. Maybe that is why a lot of people liked me is because my humor was so bizarre. Every one had fun except my oldest brother, he was always paranoid that some one was going to get into trouble and were going to loose our house. My oldest brother was always good for that. He worried himself sick even for a mere $700. Oh well I have always told him that you're never going to start living your life until the Doctor tells you have six months to live. Any ways back to the grad party. When the ceremony was done, a lot of my class mates came back to my house. When it was around 10:30, my dad said that the party was going to start winding down however; he did have two kegs at the liquor store for me to pick up. Around 11:30 the party moved to Little Bad Waters. We partied there all night until the next day. I remember a good friend of mine jack had taken me to his car; he had about a ½ oz. of some great pot. We smoked a lot of it. I remember barb being there too with us getting high. There must have been about 20 people there, all of my good friends. The next thing I remember is a graduated class mate of mine being there. I was never friends with her; I never really ever even talked to her or hung out with her. All that I remember is that we were away from every one deep in the woods, as she was taking her clothes off wanting to have sex, so did I. as we were laying on the ground naked I asked her " do you wanna have sex with a real experienced guy"? She said yes I want you. So I fucked the living hell out of her, for at least a good hour or two. That was the only time I fucked her or seen of her. She may as well have a child of mine. It kind of reminds me of the movie The Breakfast Club. Two complete strangers getting together. Now after I got back to the party, we drank all night, I can't remember everything, but it must have been around 9:00AM when it was done I was so hammered I got into a friends car Pugsley. I remember us fishtailing and then like wham! We went into the ditch. I remember my head hitting the windshield. Another friend tom had went off of the road also, but managed to get back on. We pulled Pugsley's car out of the ditch. I didn't drive with him. As he drove away, his car just fishtailed down the road. We ended up back at Andy's apartment. I crashed there for awhile. Later on in the afternoon Kurt, Glen, and I went fishing at Big Bad Waters.

A couple of weeks later, I had to go to court, (remember with the drinking and driving episode)? I was sentenced to two weeks in jail, plus go to alcohol counseling, fines, court costs all that good stuff. Two weeks seemed like an eternity. This one night as I was lying in my bed, this vision of a hand came out of the sky and a voice said to me "Jason, you can't keep doing what you are doing it will kill you". Then it went away. I didn't know what to make of it. I thought no way. I blew it off. When I got out, I remember it was a Sunday, and I had to meet my parents. We went to camp and my dad and I had started to help him on the camp. The next day an album that I have been waiting for was finally being released ACE FHREHLEY'S COMET came to stores. I couldn't wait for it. I remember being in my room and playing the song "Rock Soldiers" when it was about ¾ of the way done, I fell to the ground on my knees. I heard that voice again in jail and I started to cry. I seen my life flash before me and all the times I cheated death. I knew I had to stop doing what I was doing, otherwise it will kill me. I was confused, I felt alone for the first time in a long time. What do I do? I got really depressed, to the point of suicide. I can't remember when it happened, but Barb and I broke up. I think it was in the summer though. I had gone out with a girl named Lisa; she was from Iron Mountain School. She actually was a nice girl. We didn't last long. I still had my drinking buddies, and I did drink, but I knew I had to get rid of them both. If you have never had a nervous break down, it isn't fun. I had one and I hated it. I was still living crazy, but I was cutting back. I had to go to alcohol counseling; there I met a really nice lady. She was really great, so great that I had an inspiration; I wanted to help people with problems. I decided to be a social worker. I had a lot of people laughed at me for wanting to do that. But then now that I look at it years later, look at who I was hanging around with. It is now 2007 I don't have any of the friends that I used to have. And it feels great. All of the people that I have seen some have gone on to reach new heights in their lives. Some of them are fuck- ups still drinking and doing drugs, and have never got anywhere in life. Some have straightened up. One thing what was scary for me was the separation from high school to adult life. I think some people can't handle this, and they eventually committing suicide. I remember living up at camp with my friend Andy. I remember having a nervous breakdown because of the separation. What am I going to do? I was totally shit scared of what I was doing. Andy and I would take many rides to Bay College expecting to find out about classes. It took a long time for me to feel good about what I was doing. Then one day I had to meet with a college counselor Jim Peterson; he told me because of my poor academic grades, for my trying to attend this school, I'd be running with a broken leg. That dick ruined me and my desire for helping people. I slipped into a deep depression. He talked me into going to college for art and design. In 1989, I graduated from bay in what I didn't want to. My first year in college was scary. I think it's scary when you don't have parents who never took you under their wing in that type of environment. My kids since they were born have been to Bay College and NMU a bunch of times. They know they will be in college. I remember the day before school started January 8th, 1988 I remember walking to my dorm and up the stairs to my room. This was really fucking scary for me. I remember crying on my bed, and I played a song by Alice Cooper Were All Crazy. I thought I was crazy for being here. I thought of packing my stuff up and quitting. I didn't although I went and I got almost straight A's in school. I have even won two scholarships; Alice Powers Memorial, and The Bay Bank Scholarship, and I graduated in 1989 with a degree I didn't want all because I listened to people. I quit school, even though I wanted to be a social worker, and I never returned until years later. I was still drinking and smoking, but at a more lower level.

In 1990 a girl friend and I went to see KISS in Green Bay. As we were in the mall, I ran into ERIC CARR, the drummer of KISS. I showed him pictures of my room and he asked me what I did for a living? I broke down and cried, he asked me what's wrong? I told him what happened in college and what I wanted to do. He told me what KISS stood for, and I guess I never really listened to what the music stood for. Well I didn't go to college until 1992. My first class was intro to psych. I got an A+. I did go back on a slower course, but I made it. At this time it was hard to go to college, with kids, and especially a wife who doesn't want you to go and when you have to work full time, take care of kids, and the house. My first wife was a real screw up, we got divorced in 1996. I was then able to go to college full time. In 1995 I had to move back with my parents when we split. I hated it. It reminded me of living at home with the abuse when I was a kid. My older brother is a complete know it all. He was good at terrorizing my kids, he done a good job at it with me. I hated it. In the fall of 1996 I left home because of my mom and my older brother. I think the only thing my first wife did that was good for me was kids, and I got a closer relationship with my dad. My job that I had was working for The Dickinson County Juvenile Probate Court. Oh man I love that job. I love working with kids. One day the Honorable Judge Robert G. Foster Took my kids into his chambers, and showed him what a Judge does. It was fun. In 1999, I graduated with an associate degree in Human Services. That was a really enjoyable day and a great accomplishment. My dad, the boys and I went to Herford & Hopps for a burger. I even had a beer, just one. I could finally enjoy the taste of beer and not for getting drunk. In the fall of 1999 I had went on to NMU to receive four degrees in 2002: I have received a Sociology Degree, Social Work Degree, Human Services Degree, and an Education Degree. Wow! I finally did it. I can't believe what I had done; it is like a dream come true. And to think I done this despite three back operations, Suffering from Bi-Polar, Severe Depression, Severe Mood Disorder, Benign Tremors, Learning Disabled, ADD, and also having Severe Asthma. Having being told I'd never make it, I was wasting my time. I have been working with troubled kids, and I was approached by the D&R, they want to know if I would be interested in teaching Hunter Safety to kids as well. Hummmmm I might just do it.

If there is one thing that I learned is to take people's advice with a grain of salt. Don't believe every thing you hear. You be the judge. Most people that I have talked with said that I should have been either dead, committed suicide, or in prison. But yet these people don't realize that the best counselors are the ones that were alcoholics who are recovering, people who were abused, or who had other addictions or problems. Even I a recovering alcoholic just as severe depression, it is something that I am battling every day. But it is getting better with age. Today 2007 I can drink just one beer. If I try to drink more than that, I get really sick, vomit, and get sleepy. I learned this from my alcoholic teacher in college; it is known as a "reverse tolerance". At this time my oldest child Mike is a freshman at Rapid River High School. He is a well respected musician 1st chair in the French horn. He also plays foot ball for Rapid River, and is in the Science Olympiad. Marcus he is also a Basket Ball player of the 8th grade team, he is also motocross dirt bike racer, last year he cut his foot wide open, we thought he was going to loose his foot. That was quite an experience, but he took it like a man. One nurse was so impressed with him; Marc had to sign one of his racing jerseys and gave it to her. All of my kids get above average grades. They have a lot more involved parents than what I had. This makes me believe that this is the biggest payoff. I think if my kids really knew what I had done during my school life, I think they would be shell shocked.

In closing: Some people don't think I have gone very far, I argue other wise. I think it has a lot to do with motivation and what you're willing to put up with to get what you want. Some people say I've pushed the envelope. Some want to know how I done it. Some told me to write a book, ok. And some people ask me if there was anything in life, what would I have changed, or done differently. Just let life take its course, I have had so much fun doing the things I done. I really appreciate the sexual experiences I had and the parties. I guess I am one lucky son of a bitch that walked the face of the earth for the things I've done. I think the only thing I would like to do is create more chaos and fun. But I can honestly say if I was to die today, I sure had fun.

Chapter three:
Experiencing life

THE WOMEN!!!! Well of all the chapters I write, this has to be one of my favorite that I have done. I just grasp my hands and think of what I have done and I must say that I am one lucky son of a bitch to have walked the face of the earth. I have a big Rubbermaid container of pictures and things that I have save from over the years, and I appreciate it very much and do rummage through it once in a while. I have everything from pictures, to letters, clothing, jewelry, cards, and a whole bunch of other stuff. As I start to type it feels like I'm taking a journey back in time to a magical place that I will always remember….. I can honestly say that I have slept with 30 women in my life time. Some would say I should be ashamed, but I am not. I have had a lot of fun that I will forever cherish.

Rochelle was a really cool girl. I had met at the roller rink in Iron Mountain, Mi. It was a Saturday night and a friend Ray, who I was living with at the time, went out that night. We had bought some beer, it was easy to get alcohol in those days, just hop over to Wisconsin and walla you can get anything there you like. Any ways we were both fucked up by the time we got to the rink and it was quite humorous trying to skate while drunk. As I was going around and around, I seen this girl that went to my school, and I wanted her in the worst way. I knew I had to talk to her so I made an emergency stop, wipe out all over the floor and taking a bunch of kids down with me. I made my way over to her and she was there with a friend Terri, who I knew, so it was easier to break the ice and I started to talk to her. We talked for a while and I asked her out and she said yes. This was so cool to me here I am gonna take out a girl that I was infatuated with. I found out that she lived at Rivers Bend, which was just a skip away from Ron's house.

The next day, Ray and I were riding out three wheelers on Bass Lake and it was like dejavu Rochelle and her mom were riding on the lake in her car, I drove across to where they were and I talked to them. She told me where she lived and within an hour I was at her house.

By the middle of next week Rochelle and her friend Liz came over to our house. Liz wanted to go out with Ray, who was a friend of Rochelle made all the moments better. I had been living at Ray's house for about a month now. I've been having some problems at my own house, so there I am. I remember the bedroom closet Ray had, it was quite big, so we decided to put some small speakers in there in case if you needed a private place to be, and boy that was needed. We both got in there and we were kissing and then feeling each other. She took off her shirt and boy did I have some fun. Soon after she undone my pants and after that I knew I was in for. I highly suspect that it became apparent to Ray and he did the same.

For the life of our relationship, all I wanted to do was be with this girl and I can't remember when but I ended up moving back home. I can say honestly that it wasn't that I came from a poor family, I got everything I wanted: three wheelers, ATV's a boat, cars, and trucks. It's just that I knew there wasn't much love there. That's what bothered me. And I got to do what ever I wanted to. I remember on the following Friday taking Rochelle back to my house and my parents being gone and just screwing the hell out of her. Man this was heaven to me. We would go to my room and jam out to KISS music, getting high and totally drunk and getting laid whenever I wanted. This roller coaster lasted for about six months. We broke up I'm not sure why, but she was one of the first girls who I did coke with. I know now it's nothing to brag about. But at the time it was fun. We parted our ways and she ended up moving to California.

Sheba was my next girl I met. I had a party at my parents house, like I said I got to do anything I wanted to and I don't know how or why she came there, I never knew her, but any ways she was there. Can you imagine what it is like to be throwing a beer party with your parent's home? At a lot of situations that have happened, I can't quite recall how things started, so bare with me. I don't know how or why but we ended up going out that night.

On the following Saturday afternoon I had made plans to pick her up at the Big Boy Restaurant. In there I was patiently waiting for her drinking coffee. She came in and I knew in my heart I was gonna slay this girl today. We got back to my house and by this time my parents had just gone to church, so no one was home. There was a famous song by Deep Purple called "No one's home, my belly is aching" she would sing that song. I guess she was hungry. This was the second girl I had in my bed room. And for those of you, who knew me, remember my room was a KISS Shrine. And like before she would come over to my house on Saturday and have all kinds of fun. It even got to the point where she would come home with me after school and fuck in my room. This girl was like the ultimate. I did her in my room, at my camp, her camp, in cars, just anywhere. Believe it I would even leave my house on Friday, and sleep over her house and in her bed until

Sunday night. Her dad and I got along quite well. He was a serious alcoholic and we would drink constantly. I can remember drinking up at their camp with him. One night I got so fucked up that her mom had to drag me across the floor and tuck me into bed. That happened many times during this relationship. I was with this girl for a while. She wanted to get married and have kids. I wanted that too, but I knew I was in no shape to have kids. I remember one time when I used to work at Lake Antoine Park, I ran into this chick that lived by me and she had a cousin Char, who wanted to have a good time. I was supposed to meet Shelia after work, but yet this new girl was waiting for me now. I called Sheba from a pay phone and told her I was really sick and I was going home, she wanted to come and take care of me, but I said no. When work got done , Char got on my three wheeler and we rode off to my house to where I called Sheba and told her I was going to bed. Char and I went to the liquor store and picked up a case of beer and I got my sleeping bag, and we drank for a good time talking and getting to know one another. I found out that she was from Chicago and a complete slut, which was ok for me. So we banged at the Moon Lake Base Ball Park for the whole night.

Even though I did this, for the first time, and two I didn't like what I was doing to Sheba. She ended up finding out what happened but forgave me. I thought to myself I couldn't do that again so I decided to get serious with her and talk about marriage. I knew or I thought I'd never be able to go to college, (or os I thought so) I decided to go into the Military. The US NAVY was what I wanted to go into and since I was good at welding, that would be my field of experience. Well to make the story short, I didn't get in to the NAVY due to asthma problems. I know that those of you who knew me, I kept a pretty good job of hiding my asthma condition. I will explain this more in depth in a later chapter. It seems that after I couldn't get into the NAVY, Sheba and I just fell apart. I had another affair on her with a girl named Rose. I can't remember how I met her either, but I remember my friend Bob was driving my car and we were banging in the back seat. And at this time I was avoiding her at all costs. I remember Sheba came out to my ice shack on BIG BAD WATERS and she was upset and I kept drinking to kill the pain, that is one of the cowards of alcohol, it can suppress your feelings, but I didn't care that I was breaking her heart, so bad that in time she left me for her new found husband. And I guess she has a bagel shop. Good for you Sheba I am so happy for you.

Raised number one I am sorry to inform you that I can't tell you how many times we were together, but it was a short lived romance.

I remember this Christmas mixer we had at school, a friend of mine Candy had another girl with her Kelly she was very interested in me. I actually had to go to the dance with her. Before the day was done she was telling me that she loved me. I can remember she was at my ice shack along with her brother, and a good friend Glen. I remember us drinking and I was fingering her and her brother was sitting across from us in the shack. I never did have sex with this girl, but it was her sister Barb that my brother took out and came to a beer party we had at the Bad Water Sandpits. I remember it was early spring and he had dropped her off at the party and left. I knew for some reason it didn't work out between them, so she hung out with me. It was some time after that the party got busted so we left and went to Rick's house, where we partied until the early morning. We went back to the sandpit drinking and listening to the radio. Barb made the moves on me and undone my button and zipper on my jeans. She completely got stripped down and we banged all night. She was 20 and I was 18. I thought this was cool being with an older chick. We banged every where, even behind the school. This was the first time that one of my parents objected to a girl I was with. My parents have had no clue on what kind of a kid I was like. And they never will as long as I can help it. Barb and I have gone to a couple of concerts. I remember one time we went to see Ratt and Poison in Marquette. It was a hot day and we had a cooler full of beer. We sat on the top of the hood of my car listening to tunes, sucking on some suds, and taking in the son. The cops came by in an unmarked car and made us dump out our beer. That was fine, since the cooler was in the car. Just get another one. Even though I liked this girl, I knew she was a tramp, and a hard ass. I had made her go to Shelia's house and get my 10 speed. I really liked it and I wanted it back and she wouldn't give it up. Well I got it back. HA HA. This was the girl that had gone out on me several times, it hurt, but I kept coming back for more. She was the girl who also was pregnant with my kid; she called me one day and wanted to talk to me, so I met her at the gas station in Kingsford, where she said she was pregnant. I was scared for once on a long time. I didn't tell my parents, I wanted to wait until as long as possible. She was on a boat on Lake Antione and this guy made a sharp turn and she lost her balance and hit the side of the boat with her belly, causing her to have a miscarriage. Even from this day, my parents never knew of this and I never would tell them either. I know that it wasn't very long and we had broken up, and she had moved to Colorado. I did run into her in 1990 in Norway working at a gas station. She wanted to get together, but I said no due to the fact she was married. I did however run into to her dad Willard, where I was returning some pop cans for Boy Scouts and I guess she lives in Athelstane, WI. He showed me some of her kids, but I am too afraid to pursue to see if any of them are mine. I often wondered if she told me a lie and that she was still pregnant.

Mich: I met this girl in 1987 at the Bad Water Bridge. I've been drunk many time coming over that bridge. We actually met from an old girlfriend and that we decided to park out at the Little Bad Water Party spot. And on the first night we fucked to our hearts content. We were together for three years, which gave me a real wake up call. I started to go to college and she would come up there and spend lots of night there with me. This girl was actually the one I was with, that I wanted to stop drinking. She still wanted to party, but I didn't. I was still smoking a lot of pot and I can honestly say drinking too, but I was phasing out with it. She and I went to many concerts, and even a Green bay Packer Foot Ball game. That was fun. She met Eric Carr of KISS, and almost met Gene Simmons too. I can remember many times her parents would go out of town, and I would spend the weekend with her and fuck all weekend long and the same when my parents would go to church. A lot of women that I had were in my room when my parent's went to church. She also thought she was pregnant too, but I told her not to tell her parents until she knew for sure. Well she wasn't what a relief. This was at the ending of our relationship. This was also the ending of me being a kid. You see along with her and all of the other girls I was with. I was never honest about myself, having health problems. This was also the time when I got into my first car accident, which would lead me to many back operations down the road. We broke up and I knew in the long run it was because of me. And it hurt because it wasn't fair.

I had many one night stands since Mich, I remember this certain girl Theresa, and we were over by the Lake Antoine Sand Pit, where we fucked in my new truck. She really wanted to be with me for the long term, but I thought it was too soon since she wanted me to get her pregnant on the first night. At this time in my life I could see differences in the classes of people. This girl really tried to butter me up, but it didn't work. All what I could see with this girl is a life of bad luck.

Sheba #2 yes I had many girls with the same name, but what was so funny about this relationship, is that she was living in the same house on the North Side of Iron Mountain that my ex- girlfriend Sheba #1 was living in. it was kinda hard having sex in the same house especially when Sheba #1 wrote on her bedroom wall Sheba & Jason., and screwing Sheba#2 at the same time. She and I did actually get to go to a couple of KISS concerts. One was in Marquette, and the other the next day was in Green Bay. We didn't last long and we parted our ways.

I've had two one night stands with two girls that graduated in the class of 1987. I will not reveal any names. I will say that they got the rocking of a life time.

Cherry my x wife: I am gonna keep this short as possible. We met at her house, she had a party there. I wasn't really drinking much. I will tell you more on that later. Things just unfolded and by the end of the night we were in bed. The next day I went home. I wanted to be with her, but I didn't want to put up with the drinking. She called me later that evening saying she made me a nice dinner. I went there and I told her that I didn't like the drinking, and she told me she wasn't into to it either. And she was tired of the drinking scene. Well finally, I thought to myself that I finally found a person who was on my level. She had three other kids who I took as my own, they even called me dad. We soon had two kids of our own Michael & Marcus. Every other girl I was with I didn't want to get pregnant, but this girl I felt it was right. What I thought was kinda cool is that when I married her, I was also related to a few kids in my graduating class. Well any ways we did get married in 1992, and we were married until 1996. Like I said I was going to make the story short. After six months of marriage, things started to change. I noticed money missing in our bank account, for which she said "the bank must have made a mistake". I found myself trying to keep a 40 hour a week job and keep the house up, and taking care of kids. The very last day we were together, she was acting very weird, I never seen someone acting like this. She told me that she didn't want to be with me no more. It felt relieving to me for her to say that. She told me that she was doing crack, crank, coke, pot;

so I guess this explains for the odd behavior. I can't quite remember what happened but I then remember her grabbing a knife and I told the next door neighbor to call 911 and then Cherry came after me with a vengeance. She came after me with a knife calling me a basterd. She tried to hit me, but I grabbed her arms, so she couldn't hit me but she broke her free and hit me in the mouth. The cops soon arrived and she was arrested, and in jail where she belongs. We got divorced in1996 and I have had sole custody of my boys.

After my divorce, I moved back to my parents where I had my boys. I stayed there from fall till the next fall where I moved back to my home. At this time I met a girl "G". I had met her in college and I thought for myself this must be the right girl for me. She owned her own house, like me. And was working and taking care of her. We dated for a while and then she moved into my house. It didn't take too long for me to figure it out this was going to be a disaster. First off she had this dog that would piss on the floors of my house and to tell you the truth it really pissed me off. I've tried to correct it from doing it, but it wouldn't stop. Finally one day I told her it's me or the dog, and she told me that she couldn't make up her mind that quick. She has been through too much with that dog and that she's even ruined relationships because of that dog. I felt like telling her that well now you've ruined another one too. I could see from the start that this relationship was going nowhere but down hill. I've went through a lot of bullshit with this girl. She kept pushing me to have kids and get married, and I kept stalling her. She even tried to make me go to counseling and to have the counselor tell me to start having kids, but once the counselor knew what I had went through with my x wife, she said "don't you see what he has went through". We broke up after three years. Whew.

Lacy: this girl I met at Bay College back in 1989. She had a friend Connie who really liked to be with me. I never really dated her, but she was a nice person to be with if you know what I mean.. Now lets roll ahead a decade, ok its now 1999 and I was going to Northern Michigan University for my Bachelors Degree in Social Work. This is where I met Lacy again, and she looks just as beautiful as before. I remember saying hi to her in the hall, but I knew she didn't remember me. I just kept thinking about the first time I met her. Then the unthinkable happened, we had a class together. And for some reason, we talked together and got along really fine. I don't think neither of us knew that we were to be wed and to live happy. We did a lot of fun things when we first met; like go out to eat, go to concerts, and our kids all four of them Lacy had two kids too got along extremely well. But reality set in for the both of us, if you remember I have some health problems, asthma, back problems. And little did I know that she has some problems too. I remember the day we were in her car and she looked over to me and saying" we can't keep going on like this". "I want to tell you something you must know". And I said ok tell. She looked at me with those sultry eyes and said "I really like you but must know something, I have MS- multiple Sclerosis" and then she said to me "can you live with that"? And all I thought was WHEW!!!! What a relief, because I told her of the health problems I have and it was just like everything fell in place. In 2000, I moved to her house and in 2002 we both graduated from NMU. In 2006 we built a brand new house. We have accumulated a mass of a lot of material things.

I can't believe that I have finally found some one who really loves me for who I am. I and I can love some one for who they really are too. Now if you remember how with all of the other girls except Cherry; Lacy I feel just the same about having kids with, and I also feel relaxed about sharing a bank account with too. I guess love can really happen to you, you just have to be patient and waiting. Lacy and I got married on December 26, 2000. And I have been happy ever since. That is as long as the depression can stay away, but like a monster it took over me through out the years, and lacy couldn't take it no more of me and she wanted a divorce. I REALLY WANT TO SAY THANK YOU TO MY PARENTS FOR ALL OF WHAT THEY HAVE NOT DONE, AND TO MY BROTHERS FOR THE ABUSE BOTH PHYSICALLY AND MENTALLY, AND ALSO TO ONE FAMILY MEMBER FOR MOLESTING ME. I SURE HOPE YOUR QUICK FIXES HAVE LEFT ME WITH A LIFE LONG LEGACY OF PROBLEMS, OR IN OTHER WORDS "THE ENDLESS PRICE I HAVE TO PAY". Lacy and I are currently getting a divorce, which will be granted on 8 - 10-07. Believe me in all, she is a beautiful person, but that is ALL she got. She took me by surprise and with out warning. It was Memorial Day Weekend; we went to see a movie with the kids and in laws. Saturday, I built a deck for her parents. Sunday we went to Marquette and she showed me around to where she lived. My dad had come over for lunch. On Monday, she asked me for a divorce. It has been a total shock to me. I don't understand what I could have done. This is a definite learning lesson. You can get very depressed, and live in depression, or you can move on. Learning the skills that I know, I will move on. She did send me to a nervous break down, and like a good case of the runs; she was out of my system in five days.

To any of you out there who are going through a break up, Please understand this will come to pass. It is not the end of the world. I know it might feel like it is now, but believe me things will get better. Consider it as your own to hell and back.

In closing, some people think I should be ashamed of what I've done, but actually maby my parents should be ashamed of what they have done. I am not mad just confused my life is like a compass spinning out of control of its direction and emotions. And even if it did stop, I wouldn't know where to turn.

Chapter four:
My best friend, my hunting buddy I miss you so much

When I was in 7th grade, I met a friend named Devin. He was a friend of my older brothers. He lived about 2 miles away from me, so it was easy to visit. This was great he lived close by and it felt nice to have a friend. Devin was more than just a friend; he was like a big brother to me. I always wanted to fish; my dad never took me out fishing, or did things like a parent or brother would do. He did. He taught me all the know how to be a good fisherman, and a good hunter, that my dad never did with me either. The only thing odd about us is that he was 8 years older than me. I was born in 1968, and he was born in 1960, so there was quite an age difference, still we liked to do stuff. And I had some one to do it with. We drank, smoked and were merry. I remember one night in 1981; we were at his dad's house by Bad Waters. We bought some beer and decided we would shoot a deer. At around six PM, Kevin shot a nice big doe, we sat around for an hour drinking and then we went out gut it and bring it back. It was pitch dark with just a little flashlight to work with, but we got the deer. We decided to double back, so we wouldn't get caught. This was the first time I've ever driven a vehicle drunk, and not the last time either. Who ever reads this book, please don't drink and drive. We pulled up in the drive way and went to bed. When we got up, I had made the mistake of driving the truck nose in. I should have backed it in. luckily no one drove by, so we backed it in and started to process the deer, and drink beer.

Another thing I loved to do was fish and boy did Devin too. We caught many fish, and he taught me well. One time in the very early spring in 1982, we decided

59

to take the boat out. We launched at the Bad Water Bridge, on to the Menominee River. We drove about two miles up stream to do some Walleye fishing. It was a nice morning and we thought we would try our luck. We caught a lot of fish and when dusk started to set in, we decided to go home. Devin started the boat motor, we went about 20 feet, and the bottom gear of the boat broke. We had to row almost two miles. I remember the weather getting nasty, with snow, and force winds would push the boat against the iced up sides of the river. We had no lights or anything; we thought we were going to die. It seemed like it was taking for ever. If we were going to die then just get it over with. I don't know how long it took, but we did reach the boat landing. We were lucky to have gotten out of that mess.

Devin and I loved to ice fish we did a lot of that too. We would spend the night on the ice; fishing catching lots of Northern Pike. One year I remember in 1982, during this year, we didn't get much snow. As a matter of fact, we didn't get hardly any at all. This one time fishing, I remember us having a big spread of lines out. If a tip – up went up, we would ice skate to inspect it. That was a lot of fun, and we caught a lot of fish. I must say that we did a lot of fishing and drinking when we were together. We were quite inseparable to say the least. He was like a big brother as I have said. I remember one time we were ice fishing in his shack and we were talking a lot and I remember Devin diving down toward the ice hole, as the fishing pole was going under and to my surprise, he pulled out a monster northern pike I'd ever seen. We also used to fish at this one shack at bad waters, which was made into the ground. An old guy named Ernie gave it to Devin a long time ago, and Devin gave it to me. This shack was placed there in 1963 that's where we fished the most, and I continued to fish there until 1988. After that I haven't been there since until 2000, I took a snowmobile ride over to it, and someone had smashed it and pushed it into the lake. I do want to get back over there again and pay a sort of homage to my friend. I would remember the fish that the very first one of the season, we would nail it to the ice shack. I often wonder if it was due to the fact we had depression, was that the reason which kept us close. I know all was not good; one time Devin and his girlfriend and I went out cruising, which was drinking and driving. They were fighting and the next thing I remember Devin was out of the car and beating up his girlfriend. Of course I got involved and did what I could do to stop him from beating her up. Some one called the police, and back in those days they never took spousal abuse seriously. This was in 1982, now if this was to have been in 2000; I would have gotten an MIP, drunk driving, assault, and being thrown in jail. How times have changed. I even seen him take a buck knife and stab his stomach and watch it bleed. He always talked of killing himself; I wonder if that is where I got it from? I definitely done a lot of crazy shit for my age, but remember my parents never cared about what I did or done. We did have some fun times, like we would often go bowling almost every Saturday night. That was fun things that my parents never did with me. One time I remember we went to the movies, we seen Rambo First Blood. That was like wow! What a cool movie. I still watch it when I can. Devin took care of me like a big brother/ dad figure. I always looked foreword to cruising at night with him, we mostly around the Bad Waters area, and we usually got a 12 pack for the ride. He got me into the rock band Rush. I remember in 1981 he played a cassette Rush Moving Pictures. I was totally blown away by them. They are like a close second favorite. He was the one who I am thankful for , for learning how to tie a fisherman's knot, hook a minnow in the right way, how to dress a deer, where to shoot a deer and make it count. How to skin a deer, dress and prepare a duck, clean, prepare and, identify fish he taught me it all. Now I can and have taught it to my kids.

One of the worst days of my life happened to me in May 31, 1983. I found out that my friend had committed suicide. I went into a deep, deep depression, which nobody recognized or seemed to care. I remember sitting in my room and listening to music and just crying. I tried to commit suicide many times, but thankfully never succeeded. Thank God. I still miss him I often think what would it be like if he were around? He would be out fishing, or shooting ducks with my boys. Maybe there is a reason why he is not here. I wish you were here. Since writing this chapter, I am going to place a wood duck house in the area where that ice shack once stood still. There will be a metal engraving that will say "in loving memory of Devin ******** 5- 17 -83. Every time when I go duck hunting, and when it is calm, as the sun starts to break the sky. I watch my decoys move gently in the wind. It always reminds me that Devin is with me.

Chapter five:
My most cherished friend
Jake. A friend every one
should have

My best friend
And other friends

If there was ever a friends a great as Devin, Jake is he. I met him out duck hunting. He was actually hunting in the place where I had been hunting. It was funny as I came around the corner, I seen a bunch of mallards. Whenever I walk to the blind, I never load my gun, it is always cased. So here I am trying to load my gun, then all of the sudden he pops out of the sticks. Whew! Like oh man I almost shot your decoys dude. I don't know if any of you out there duck hunt, but there is certain camaraderie among hunters, a special friendship and bonding. One day during duck season, I took a ride to the boat landing, and there was this old guy who was getting ready to hunt. I never met this guy, but in about 10 minutes, he was in my truck smoking a cigar wanting to know when and where going to go hunting. That's what I mean about duck hunters. With Jake I haven't even known him for but a couple of months. In about three months, we have hunted many times; we have shown each other our hot hunting spots. We have created a duck club called DELTA DUCK CLUB. It is a club where we clean and preserve wet land habitat. In February of 2007, we will be on the radio with real sportsman called THE OUTSPOKEN SPORTSMAN. And then later in the spring, we will be on TV6 Discovering Show. I know there will be much more to come in the future. Like I said I haven't known Jake for very long, but I know we will have a beautiful friendship for YEARS to come.

Grizzley: this is the guy who I told you who I met with the cigars. Every bit of that story is true. This man is 75 years old and still pushing a boat out to hunt ducks. He told me that when he started to hunt, the daily limit on ducks was 100. Holy cow! No wonder why there are lower numbers of birds today. It's sad but true. One thing that I love about hunting with older people is the stories that they have to say. I just enjoy them. I know that one day I will be the one telling the old stories. It kind of makes me sad that one day the sun will set on me too. One day I too will hang my gun on the rack for the last time.

Abe is another friend who duck hunts. We actually met through Boy Scouts. We've been friends for about two years now. We have hunted lots and took lots of ducks. He and I have built three nice duck blinds. We do a lot of ice fishing too along with Nate as well. You know it's nice to have friends that don't revolve around drinking.

Kent: he and I have been friends for a good 30 years by now. We did a lot of hunting and fishing, and ice fishing mostly done with alcohol and pot. We had so many good times together; I could write a book on just that. Although I have moved away from him, I still see him from time to time.

Dan: what can I say I'm speech less? We did so much drinking and drugs. He is another book. He was my best man at my first wedding. I haven't seen him since 1994. He did call me last summer 2006 from our camp, where my brother stays. I guess my friend is real fucked up. He was driving semi, but some one had told me that he was found drunk in the cab, so he lost his license. All I can say is good luck.

Devin: he was the one who got me into hunting and fishing. He was the original one to get me started in duck hunting and I'd say I got hooked. I shot a lot of deer, and caught a lot of fish. Man we had fun. We always drank beer and just had a good time. We even violated a bunch of deer. One time we were out ice fishing, Devin and I had 70 setlines in Big Bad Water. Could you imagine if we got caught? Wow! What a fine we'd have to pay. I know we drank beer, but he is the only friend that I wish wasn't dead. I really miss him. Every time when I go duck hunting, and when it's a sunny morning. As the sun starts to break the sky and the decoys are moving gently. I feel that Devin is there with me. This happens every time. I can't explain it. I wish you were here bud. I sure miss you.

All the other fuck ups I have detached myself from and I don't know where they are in life, what they do in life and I really don't give a dam. It's kind of sickening that I have over 10 friends who have killed themselves, either by using a gun, or by overdosing. I understand from the point of looking at them from a counselor's perspective. But what I really feel like saying is where in the hell were the parents in their lives? I guess I must be the lucky one. Believe me I am happy for it every day. My parent's never got me out of it; I got myself out of it.

Chapter six:
High times and concert fun

CONCERT JOURNEYS:

Concerts to me were like the jocks going to a foot ball game. We both got fired up. When I was just a little kid, I always loved going to the Sportsmans Club especially when there was a wedding. I loved to go and watch the band. It's a far cry from today, now there are cd's and Dj services. I feel there is no talent in that. I was introduced to music in 1974. Sky hooks, Alex Harvey to name a few. Back in them days we 8 tracks. In 1975 I was introduced to a band named KISS. I instantly fell in love with them. Everything was Kiss. Kiss. Kiss. I had every album, and 8 track. Then in 1977, KISS was doing a concert in Green Bay, WI. I really wanted to go, but I had no one to take me. The only thing I could do was watch channel 2 news and Chuck Ramsy was at the air port, the KISS jet was flying over, getting ready to land. Then at the 10:00 news I guess some one had gotten trampled at the show. Man I wish I could have went. Oh well life goes on. In 1983 KISS was playing in Milwaukee, WI I wanted to go real bad and at this time I was able to go. I went to the show with two other kids, except they were in the 12th grade. We all got along great. This was like the best day of my life. I am finally seeing the greatest rock band on earth. It was awesome, the opened with creatures of the night, and on this tour, they had Vinnie Vincent. He was Ace's replacement. And I thought he was very good. When he did his solo, he must have taken a half hour. Gene and Paul were coming out and they had this look on their face like "Come On". And then at the end of the show, Paul came out and ran across the stage grabbing people hands. I was fortunate enough to touch his hand. I will not say who I went with, but we did party and had fun.

In 1984 Kiss was playing in Marquette on their Anamalize Tour. My brother took me; this was about the only time we ever done anything. We drank all the way up there, and in the parking lot. WASP was the opening act. They totally blew me away wow were they fucking good. And Kiss was awesome as ever. On this tour they did a video, which was cool. I found a couple of guitar pics after the show, and I bought like a $100 worth of Kiss shirts and stuff. Mad did I get fucked up. On the way out I remember there were these women out side handing out pamphlets on satanic music. I remember standing by the lady and I took one, I then remember crashing their little stand and fucking whipping those pamphlets all over the parking lot. That's was funny.

In 1985 I had seen OZZY in Green Bay. I don't want to say with whom, but it was a great time. I was so fucked up, that I don't remember who the opening act was. I do remember on the way down, we had to go to the bathroom, so we pulled into this guy's yard and went to the bathroom on his lawn. The man came out screaming and had a camera trying to take pictures, saying he is going to call the cops. We just blew out of there laughing our asses off. Man I loved seeing Ozzy it was cool when he came on stage; he was actually in the air inside of this demonic creature. When it would open up its arms, you could see Ozzy. If you watch the video "a shot in the dark", you will know what I am talking about. Oh! Now I remember who opened up. It was Metallica. They were great; it was the master of puppets tour. They were awesome. (See what happens when you do drugs kiddies!) It was great seeing Ozzy inside this demon like thing. It opend up and every one went crazy. He done that for a couple of times, he just psyched the crowd up. He put on a really, really good show.

In 1986 I had seen Kiss with a good friend Dan. We had made our own Kiss shirts to go in with. It said Kiss War Machine. They were just cheap little t shirts, but we thought they were cool. I remember the day well, it had been snowing like crazy, and there must have been a foot. My brother dropped me off at Dan's house. And we waited for our ride. While we were waiting, we smoked a good bowl or two (I lost count). Our ride came and we were on our way. We could only drive about 45 MPH because of the snow. That was ok we partied until we got there. When we were in the parking lot, there was this kid walking by you could see he was fucked up; he actually fell to the ground by us. We just watched him. He started to turn bright pink, and then he was turning purple. He must have been there for 10 minutes. Finally some one came to his aide. The ambulance was there shortly, and took him away. Once again the opening act, I can't remember but it had Carmine Appice; he was a kick ass drummer. When Kiss was playing, the main lights had come on, and four security guards had taken Kiss off the stage. Every one was saying this sucks. Some one had told us all to leave, that some one had made a bomb threat. We still didn't leave, as a matter of face we ripped up a bunch of programs and threw them around. We eventually got escorted away. About an hour later, the concert resumed, and it was good. This was really fucking funny and cruel that we did. This one kid Carl, who was in a grade higher than me, had lost his ride back to Iron Mountain. He asked me and I told him no. well we were leaving the parking lot and there's Carl walking. We stopped and asked him if he needed a ride? He started running towards the van, we started to leave and we just left him there to freeze. He was a fuckin dick.

1986 I seen Ted Nugent, and again I can't remember the opening act. In 1987 I seen Nazareth, Reo Speedwagon, with Richard Marks I also seen Ratt, I then seen Dam Yankees, the sister Christian band. In 1988 I saw Reo Speed Wagon Rush. 1989 I seen April Wine, Rush Cinderella, White Tiger, and Faster Pussycat. I seen Kiss and met the band. 1990 I seen Kiss in Marquette one day and Green Bay the next day, 1991 Black Crows, 1995 38 Special, 1996 Kiss Reunion tour, 1997 Kiss Psycho Circus Tour, 2000 Kiss Farewell Tour.

There are other shows that I have seen, I just can't remember who and when I have seen them. I really enjoyed going to the shows. I have seen Kiss 15X. They are my favorite band. In writing this chapter, I didn't want to go to in-depth, because this is not the sole purpose.

Chapter seven:
E=MC2

"You will never get to paradise with out a fight"
Jason Murra 2008

What I learned in the last 20 years: if anything in the last 20 years has taught me is to stop listening to everyone's advice. In years back, people made up my mind for me and I can honestly say it was hard for me to do on my own, well today I do it for myself. I don't need people filling my head up with crap. They act like they know what I want, but in reality they don't know a thing about me. About the only thing they gave I was confusion and a nervous break downs. It's kind of funny in my family with my other two brothers. One acts like he has been around the world of life, but yet he has been on dry dock ALL of his life. The other one is a multi millionaire, but lives on about $4,000 a year income. He's got the world by the ass and he doesn't even know it. And then there's me. I was the first to graduate high school in 1987, I was the first to graduate from a junior college once in 1989, and then in 1999, which makes me the first to actually go to college. I was the first to graduate from NMU University in 2002 (better late than never). I was the first of the boys to have kids. I was the first of the boys to move out. I was the first of the boys to get married. I was also the first to buy a house, and the first to build a new house. And yet they think I'm a stupid mother fucker. And you know it's quite funny, when a major catastrophe occurs at my parent's house, I am usually called first. I have made many trips in the night from Rapid River to Iron Mountain.

I have left Iron Mountain in 1999. Even though there are four other siblings in my family, I personally don't feel like I have any family down there other than my dad, exception of my sister Joann; when he is gone,

I will probably never go back there. It's not that I've disowned them; I have forgiven them of what's been done. I am sure that when my oldest brother finds out that I have finally came out to confess what he did, I bet he won't have a thing to do with me or my two boys when deer hunting season comes. We just never did anything as a family, so I have chosen to let them be. I feel more of a family with Linda's family. I guess it is that family feeling I never had at home.

Don't ever let people tell who you are. You know who you are and that is the best tool you can have. Do what do you best and capitalize on it. Let yourself find out who you are. If you do what people want you to do, life won't be very much fun.

Don't let people take advantage of you, either by money, or other means that you have. Have what you got and got what you have.

Always believe in yourself, don't let people put you down for no matter what it is, or how small or big. It was hard for me to do this, but trust me it will happen.

Don't quit school no matter how bad it may get. I know there is a lot of peer pressure from other students who may want you to quit, but don't trust me it's not worth it. You will get no where in life that I will promise you. Hold it out ride out the storm, don't go down to their level, that's what they want to see happen.

Very important: GO TO COLLEGE OR THE SERVICE!!!! You really need this if you want to succeed. I know that years ago you didn't need a college education, but trust me you do in order to make some good money. Remember even if you apply for a job that has nothing to do with what you went to college for.

You will nine out of 10X get the job because what's on your résumés.

This is really important: don't get some one pregnant and like wise with the girls. Nothing that can screw up your future is getting pregnant. Wait until you are both graduated. You need a plan before you have kids. Kids should come last.

Guys: don't stay with girls that mentally abuse you especially when they want kids. As they keep harping you to have one. Trust me all that will do is cause a break up and you are stuck paying child support. Just dump them they are not worth it. And don't stay with women who want you around all of the time. You both need time. I know at first it is fun being with someone who you just met, and you will put off doing fun things like fishing, or what ever you like to do. Believe me it will get worse to the point of breakdown, it usually happens that the woman has another friend. So all you have left is wasted time not enjoying things you once did.

And people who are in relationships weather married or not, please don't do drugs especially around your kids. That is a very bad example. Do you want them to be the next drop out at 15 with a baby on the way? What kind of a life is that? Is that the kind of legacy you want to leave? And since were talking about drugs, I want you to think about this….. If you were to get caught with drugs, do you understand what kind of an emotional and financial disruption that would have on your family. Think of what you kids would go through. It's just not worth it.

I would have to honestly have to say is to take your family to church! I know when I was at home I came from a *devout Catholic parents.* (Not family). I hardly ever went to church, but I can tell you when you take your family to church, it makes life more enjoyable. I can honestly say I look fore ward going to church with my family.

Yea I would say I learned a lot in the last 20 years. The trials and tribulations should have killed me a long time ago, but God wasn't ready for me, so I guess by his means this is why I am writing this book.

I am the one who slept with your guy's girlfriends.
I am the one who put fear into your parents.

Jason Murra

Chapter eight:
The end result

If there are any of you in your life who have self doubt, and believe you can't do it; then you have given into a lower negative power. For I don't even know you and I already know you can do it.

Jason Murra 2008

Great accomplishments:
Kingsford High School 1987
Bay De Noc College 1989- Graphic Arts
1999 Bay De Noc College A.A.S Human Services
Northern Michigan University 2002 – Four Degrees
Kiwanis Ski Club 1987 to 1999 member & Secretary
Kiwanis Ski Club World Cup Board Member & Secretary
Ducks Unlimited Escanaba area Board member
Ducks Unlimited Iron Mountain Area Chairman
President and founder of Delta Duck Club Est. 2006
Boy Scouts Troop 466 Gladstone, Mi Committee Member
Assistant Scout Master Assistant Troop 466 Gladstone, Mi
When I die, I hope my duck club keeps growing. I hope to keep my Legacy alive.

Jason Murra